Amazing Heights

Samantha Bell

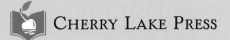
CHERRY LAKE PRESS

Published in the United States of America by Cherry Lake Publishing Group
Ann Arbor, Michigan
www.cherrylakepublishing.com

Reading Adviser: Beth Walker Gambro, MS, Ed., Reading Consultant, Yorkville, IL

Photo Credits: cover, title page: © Lorcel/Shutterstock; page 4: © Kelly vanDellen/Shutterstock; page 5: © melissamn/Shutterstock; page 7: © Licheng Huang/Shutterstock; page 8: © harissahaja/Shutterstock; page 11: © Bella Bender/Shutterstock; page 12: NPS/Patrick Myers; page 13: © WorldPictures/Shutterstock; page 14: © Kris Wiktor/Shutterstock; page 15: © Cheri Alguire/Shutterstock; page 17: © Bill45/Shutterstock; page 18: © cb_travel/Shutterstock; page 19: © DTM Media/Shutterstock; page 21: © Ale xander Petrenko/Shutterstock; page 22: © Nick Fox/Shutterstock; page 23: © Francesca Pianzola/Shutterstock; page 24: © Belikova Oksana/Shutterstock; page 25: © canadastock/Shutterstock; page 27: NPS Photo /Jacob w. Frank; page 29: NPS Photo

Library of Congress Cataloging-in-Publication Data

Names: Bell, Samantha, author.
Title: Amazing heights / written by Samantha Bell.
Description: Ann Arbor, Michigan : Cherry Lake Publishing, 2023. | Series: National park adventures | Audience: Grades 4-6 | Summary: "Take a trip to the tallest points from east to west! Which national parks have the tallest mountains? Which trees tower over the landscape? This title brings readers along to find the answers on a high interest journey to Amazing Heights. Part of our 21st Century Skills Library, this series introduces concepts of natural sciences and social studies centered around a sense of adventure"— Provided by publisher.
Identifiers: LCCN 2023010588 | ISBN 9781668927397 (hardcover) | ISBN 9781668928448 (paperback) | ISBN 9781668929919 (ebook) | ISBN 9781668931394 (pdf)
Subjects: LCSH: National parks and reserves—United States—Juvenile literature. | Mountains—United States—Juvenile literature.
Classification: LCC E160 .B448 2023 | DDC 917.3—dc23/eng/20230327
LC record available at https://lccn.loc.gov/2023010588

Cherry Lake Publishing Group would like to acknowledge the work of the Partnership for 21st Century Learning, a Network of Battelle for Kids. Please visit http://www.battelleforkids.org/networks/p21 for more information.

Printed in the United States of America
Corporate Graphics

Note from publisher: Websites change regularly, and their future contents are outside of our control. Supervise children when conducting any recommended online searches for extended learning opportunities.

Samantha Bell was born and raised near Orlando, Florida. She grew up in a family of eight kids and all kinds of pets, including goats, chickens, cats, dogs, rabbits, horses, parakeets, hamsters, guinea pigs, a monkey, a raccoon, and a coatimundi. She now lives with her family in the foothills of the Blue Ridge Mountains, where she enjoys hiking, painting, and snuggling with their cats Pocket, Pebble, and Mr. Tree-Tree Triggers.

CONTENTS

Introduction | 5

Chapter 1:
Cadillac Mountain | 6

Chapter 2:
Star Dune | 10

Chapter 3:
Yosemite Falls | 16

Chapter 4:
General Sherman Tree | 20

Chapter 5:
Denali | 26

Plan Your Adventure | 30
Modeling Mountains | 30
Learn More | 31
Glossary | 32
Index | 32

Introduction

The National Park sites help protect some of the tallest natural wonders in the United States. These include colossal mountains, towering trees, and snow-fed waterfalls. In many of these places, visitors can make their way to the top to take in amazing views. Whether it is a hike through a forest or over a massive mound of sand, these awe-inspiring heights are worth the trip.

CHAPTER 1

Cadillac Mountain

Acadia National Park, Maine

Many visitors to Cadillac Mountain in Acadia National Park are early risers. Hundreds of people make their way to the top of the mountain to see the sun come up. From October to March, Cadillac Mountain is the first place in the United States to see the sunrise. Cadillac Mountain is one of 26 mountains on Mount Desert Island. At 1,530 feet (466 meters), it is the tallest mountain in Acadia National Park. It is also the tallest mountain on the **Eastern seaboard.**

A view of the Milky Way galaxy from the peak of Cadillac Mountain in Acadia National Park

Cadillac Mountain is the first place in the United States the sun touches between October and March each year.

Although there is a road to the **summit**, visitors must hike to get to the very top. Here, the landscape is similar to that of other mountains on the island. Much of the ground is rocky. If there is soil, it is shallow and dry. Trees do not grow very tall. They may be twisted by the strong winds blowing in from the ocean. It is not surprising the island's name became Mount Desert Island.

The area around Cadillac Mountain is the homeland of the Wabanaki people, who still live there today. They are also known as the "People of the Dawnland." They hunted and fished along the coast of Maine for thousands of years. They met many European fishermen and explorers who came to the island, especially the French. In 1688, French explorer Antoine Laumet arrived. He called himself Antoine de la Mothe Cadillac. Laumet received a grant from France to establish a settlement on the island. Over the years, the mountain became a well-known landmark. Sailors on passing ships could see it from far away. By the 1800s, it had become a popular tourist stop known as Green Mountain. In 1918, the name was changed to Cadillac Mountain to honor Laumet.

A NEW START

In 1947, the weather in Maine was unusual. That summer, the state received only 50 percent of its normal amount of rain. The rains did not come in the fall, either. By October, Mount Desert Island had the driest conditions ever recorded. On October 17, a fire broke out. Winds fanned the flames, and the fire grew. It burned for a month before coming under control. It destroyed 10,000 acres (4,047 hectares) of Acadia's spruce and fir trees. When the forests regrew, other kinds of trees came in. Today, birch, aspen, and maple trees make the forests diverse and colorful.

CHAPTER 2

Star Dune

Great Sand Dunes National Park and Preserve, Colorado

Great Sand Dunes National Park and Preserve is located at the foot of the Sangre de Cristo Mountains in Colorado. The park features huge **sand dunes** that are more than 700 feet (213 m) high. Star Dune is one of the tallest sand dunes in the park. It measures approximately 741 feet (225.9 m) high from the base to the summit. But the height of the dune can change. Wind and water carry sand from the surrounding mountains to the dunes. The Ute people call the dunes "*Saa waap maa nache*," meaning "sand that moves." Smaller dunes will even move across the grasslands.

Hikers climbing Star Dune in Great Sand Dunes National Park and Preserve, Colorado

Temperatures in the park are cold in the winter and warm during the summer. Low temperatures are around –20 degrees Fahrenheit (–29 degrees C), and blizzards are common. The high temperatures reach about 80° Fahrenheit (27° C). But on sunny summer days, the temperatures on the sand can reach up to 150° Fahrenheit (66° C). Afternoon thunderstorms in July and August bring cool winds, rain, and lightning. Sometimes avalanches occur during the storms. When this happens, air is pushed through the millions of grains of sand that tumble down. This creates a natural **phenomenon** that sounds like humming. Sometimes visitors can hear a similar sound by pushing sand down the dune.

View of Crestone Peak and Mount Herard from the peak of Star Dune

A fallen tree in Great Sand Dunes National Park and Preserve

Park visitors can explore any part of the dune field. Though there is no trail, they can hike to the top of Star Dune. The hike can take from 6 to 9 hours to complete. Hikers have a variety of ways to come down. Some visitors hike the distance. Others ride down on sand sleds. Those who like to surf can try sandboarding. This sport is a blend of surfing, snowboarding, and skateboarding. However they come down, visitors seem to enjoy the trip.

A STREAM IN THE SPRING

During the winter, the Sangre de Cristo Mountains are covered with snow. As temperatures rise in the spring, the snow melts into Medano Lake. The water then flows down the mountains through the forests. By April, it starts trickling in at the base of the dunes. By May, it is a wide, shallow stream. Under the water, the sand builds up and forms ridges. The water breaks through these ridges, creating waves. By August or September, the creek has dried up again.

CHAPTER 3

Yosemite Falls

Yosemite National Park, California

Yosemite Falls is the tallest waterfall in the United States. It is located in Yosemite National Park in California. Yosemite Falls is actually made up of three waterfalls. They are Upper Yosemite Fall, the middle cascades, and Lower Yosemite Fall. Yosemite Falls drops a total of 2,425 feet (739 m). Upper Yosemite Fall drops 1,430 feet (436 m). The middle cascades drop 675 feet (206 m), and Lower Yosemite Fall drops 320 feet (98 m). The water for Yosemite Falls comes from Yosemite Creek. The creek is fed by melting snow. The flow of the waterfall depends mainly on how much snow falls and when it melts. The falls begin to flow in November.

A summertime view of Yosemite Upper and Lower Falls

A view from the Upper Yosemite Fall Trail

The water from the falls joins the Merced River. By late summer, all the melted snow has run off. Yosemite Falls is usually dry by August. But visitors can hike to the top of the falls any time of year. The trail is not easy. Yosemite Fall Trail is a 7.2-mile (11.6 kilometers) round-trip hike. The elevation increases 2,700 feet (823 m). This means that the end of the trail is 2,700 (823 m) feet higher than the beginning. The upper half of the trail is steep and rocky. But many visitors think the views from the top are worth the effort.

Depending on the season, visitors can witness some unusual sights at the falls. In the winter, ice builds up at the base of Upper Yosemite Fall. It forms a cone shape. The cone can reach as high as 322 feet (98 m), about as tall as a 25-story building. The ice usually melts by mid-April. In April and May, visitors to the falls can sometimes see a moonbow. This occurs when a full moon shines light on the base of Lower Yosemite Fall. The light is refracted in the spray of water. It creates a lunar rainbow.

WATER ON FIRE

Horsetail Fall is another waterfall in Yosemite. This small waterfall flows only in winter. It flows over the edge of a mountain called El Capitan. In February, visitors to Horsetail Fall can sometimes see another natural phenomenon. When the sky is clear, the setting sun shines behind the water. The water glows orange. When it hits the water at just the right angle, the water looks like it is on fire. This is known as the "firefall."

CHAPTER 4

General Sherman Tree

Sequoia National Park, California

Sequoia National Park in California is home to the world's largest living tree. The General Sherman Tree is a giant sequoia. It grows in an **old-growth forest** with other giant sequoias. Many of them are between 250 and 300 feet (76 and 91 m) tall. Besides being tall, they are also very big around. Some trees may be taller or wider than the General Sherman. But the General Sherman Tree is bigger than all of them in combined weight and width.

The General Sherman Tree is considered the largest living tree in the world.

A park visitor stands next to the General Sherman Tree in Sequoia National Park in California.

The General Sherman measures 102.6 feet (31.3 m) around at its base. It is 275 feet (84 m) high and still growing. Each year, the tree adds enough wood to make another 60-foot (18 m) tree. One branch of the General Sherman is almost 7 feet (2 m) in **diameter**. That is larger than most tree trunks in the eastern United States.

Scientists believe the General Sherman is approximately 2,200 to 2,700 years old. But no one knows for sure. Indigenous peoples that lived in the Sierra Nevada mountains knew about the giant sequoias. Some of the early European explorers of the 1700s mention the trees

SEQUOIA OR REDWOOD?

Giant sequoias and giant redwoods are both very tall. But there are differences. Both types of trees grow in California. However, giant sequoias grow along the western slopes of the Sierra Nevada mountains. Redwoods grow near the Pacific Ocean. Giant sequoias are larger around. Redwoods are taller and thinner. The bark of the giant sequoia is reddish brown. The bark of the redwood is a chocolate brown color. The leaves of the trees are different, too. A giant sequoia has blue-green leaves that are scale-like and sharp.
The leaves of the redwood are dark green and flat.

The General Sherman covered in snow in the winter

Two trails lead to the General Sherman Tree. You can take your pick!

in their journals. In 1852, a hunter named Augustus T. Dowd discovered a giant sequoia. News about the trees traveled fast among the settlers. But it wasn't until 1879 that the General Sherman got its name. According to the official story, fur trapper James Wolverton discovered the tree and named it. He called it the General Sherman after Army General William Tecumseh Sherman. Sherman fought on the side of the Union during the Civil War (1861–1865).

CHAPTER 5

Denali

Denali National Park and Preserve, Alaska

The highest peak in North America is Denali in Denali National Park and Preserve. Denali has an elevation of 20,310 feet (6,190 m). It is so tall that it can be seen by astronauts in space. Denali is part of the Alaska Range on the Alaska-Canada border. Denali was the original name given to the mountain by Indigenous Alaskans. They have lived on the land surrounding Denali for thousands of years. The name *Denali* means "the tall one" or "mountain-big." In the early 1900s, the mountain's name was changed to Mount McKinley after President William McKinley. But in 2015, the official name was changed back to Denali.

Denali is the highest mountain peak in North America.

One-sixth of Denali National Park and Preserve is covered by **glaciers**. They cover more than 1 million acres (404,686 ha). Glaciers begin on land until they become so heavy that they slowly flow downhill. The glaciers flow away from the mountains. The ice eventually melts into rivers. Some glaciers begin at the summit of Denali. Others drain snow and ice from the sides of the mountain. The longest glacier is Kahiltna Glacier. It is 44 miles (71 km) long down the mountain's southwestern side.

Every year, about 600,000 people visit Denali National Park and Preserve. From fall to early spring, the night skies are darker. The drier air in colder months helps

FOUR-LEGGED RANGERS

Sled dogs have worked with native Alaskans for centuries. For the last 100 years, the dogs have helped rangers in Denali National Park and Preserve. The park opened in 1917. Shortly after, in 1922, the dogs began patrolling with the rangers. Although the dogs may be slower than machines, they are more reliable. Sled dogs know the landscape. They can help navigate in bad weather. They can detect dangers hidden by ice or snow. Visitors to the park can visit the sled dog kennels. During summer, they watch the dogs do demonstrations. In winter, they can see them at work.

Denali sled dogs hard at work in the winter

make this possible. During this time, visitors have a
chance to see the Northern Lights. This atmospheric
phenomenon appears as dancing waves of colorful light.
The colors can be seen throughout the park. But most
visitors come to the park between May and September.
Some enjoy climbing the many peaks and ice walls in the
park. But to climb Denali, they need years of training
and experience. The average expedition to the top and
back takes 17 to 21 days. More than 32,000 people have
tried to climb the mountain. Just slightly more than half
reached the summit.

Activity

Plan Your Adventure!

What high places would you like to explore? Hike to the top of a mountain, slide down a sand dune, or gaze up into a giant tree. You can find even more ideas in the other books in this series. Be sure to keep a list of the places you want to visit.

Modeling Mountains

You can make a model of Denali with just a few supplies from your kitchen. Here's what you'll need to get started:

> 2 cups (473 milliliters) of all-purpose flour
>
> 1 cup (237 mL) of salt
>
> Large bowl
>
> Large spoon
>
> 1 cup (237 mL) of water
>
> Parchment or waxed paper

First, pour the flour and the salt into the bowl and stir them together with the spoon. Add the water and stir again until everything is mixed. The flour, salt, and water will become a type of dough. If the dough feels too sticky, add a little more flour. If it looks too dry, add a little more water. You should be able to pick up the dough and easily work it with your hands.

Next, look at a photo of Denali from chapter 5. Place the dough onto the parchment or waxed paper. Shape the dough into a similar form as the mountain. Notice the mountain has many peaks at different levels. You can create peaks on your mountain by pinching some of the dough.

When you have finished, leave out your sculpture to dry. Depending on how thick it is, it may take several days. When it is completely dry, you can paint it with acrylic or craft paint.

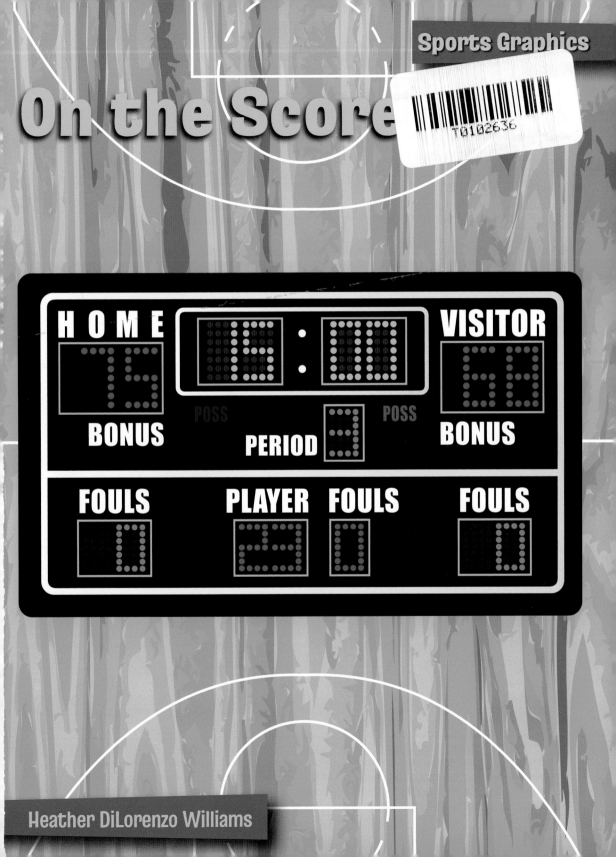

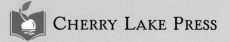
CHERRY LAKE PRESS

Published in the United States of America by Cherry Lake Publishing Group
Ann Arbor, Michigan
www.cherrylakepublishing.com

Reading Adviser: Beth Walker Gambro, MS, Ed., Reading Consultant, Yorkville, IL

Photo Credits: Cover: ©hvostik / Shutterstock; ©©artisticco / Getty Images; ©msan10 / Getty Images; ©FARBAI / Getty Images; page 5: ©Jessica Orozco; page 7: ©Jessica Orozco; page 8: ©Jessica Orozco; page 9: ©Jessica Orozco; page 10: ©Jessica Orozco; page 11: ©matsabe / Getty Images; page 12: ©Jessica Orozco; page 14: ©stevezmina1 / Getty Images; page 16: ©Jessica Orozco; page 18: ©Jessica Orozco; page 19: ©Jessica Orozco; page 21: ©Jessica Orozco; page 22: ©Jessica Orozco; page 23: ©Jessica Orozco; page 25: ©deezaat / Getty Images; page 27: ©Naomi Baker - FIFA / Contributor / Getty Images; page 27: ©ph.FAB / Shutterstock; page 28: ©Jessica Orozco

Cherry Lake Press is an imprint of Cherry Lake Publishing Group.

Library of Congress Cataloging-in-Publication Data
Library of Congress Cataloging-in-Publication Data has been filed and is available at catalog.loc.gov.

Cherry Lake Publishing Group would like to acknowledge the work of the Partnership for 21st Century Learning, a Network of Battelle for Kids. Please visit *http://www.battelleforkids.org/networks/p21* for more information.

Printed in the United States of America

Note from publisher: Websites change regularly, and their future contents are outside of our control. Supervise children when conducting any recommended online searches for extended learning opportunities.

Heather DiLorenzo Williams is a former English teacher and school librarian. She has a passion for seeing readers of all ages connect with others through stories and experiences. Heather has written more than 50 books for children. She enjoys walking her dog, reading, and watching sports. She lives in North Carolina with her husband and two children.

CONTENTS

Introduction
What's the Score? | 4

Chapter 1
Getting on the Board | 6

Chapter 2
How to Score More | 14

Chapter 3
Changing the Scoring Game | 20

Chapter 4
Who's on Top? | 24

Activity | 30
Learn More | 31
Glossary | 32
Index | 32

What's the Score?

People around the world love sports. Some go to games in person. Some watch them on television. Many people play sports in their free time. Professional athletes play for money. Sports are entertaining and great for your health. But a true sports fan knows a game is more fun when their team comes out on top.

Winning may not be everything. But celebrating a win is a lot of fun. And winning can't happen without scoring. Every sport has a set of rules for how to earn points. Whether a team scores 1 goal or 26 runs, there's only one winner when the game is over.

Four of Pro Sports' Highest-Scoring Games

FOOTBALL

WASHINGTON COMMANDERS VS. NEW YORK GIANTS
72–41, November 27, 1966 (National Football League)

SOCCER

AUSTRALIA VS. AMERICAN SAMOA
31–0, April 11, 2001 (International Soccer)

BASKETBALL

DETROIT PISTONS VS. DENVER NUGGETS
186–184, December 13, 1983 (National Basketball Association)

BASEBALL

PHILADELPHIA PHILLIES VS. CHICAGO CUBS
26–23, August 25, 1922 (Major League Baseball)

2014, Complex

CHAPTER 1

Getting on the Board

Some sports are played by a team. Soccer, baseball, and hockey are examples. Teams play against other teams. Some sports have professional players. They compete in **leagues**. Countries have teams that play in huge **tournaments**. The World Cup and the Olympics are examples of these.

Other sports are individual. These include gymnastics and figure skating. Athletes do tasks to earn points. These athletes take part in **competitions**.

Each sport has its own way to earn points. But all sports have one thing in common. Whoever has the best score is the winner!

Goal Sports

In these sports, players score by getting an object over a line or into a special area, called a goal. A goal is worth one point in hockey and soccer. In basketball, a goal is worth two or three points. A touchdown in football is worth six points.

How to Score a Game of Tennis

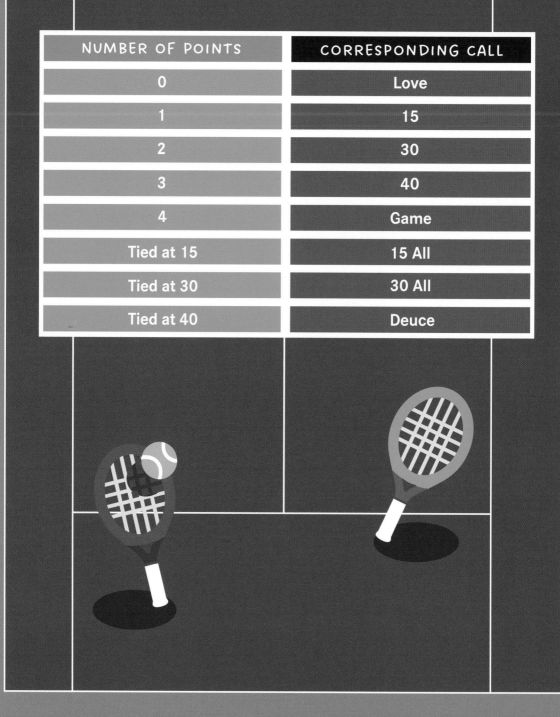

NUMBER OF POINTS	CORRESPONDING CALL
0	Love
1	15
2	30
3	40
4	Game
Tied at 15	15 All
Tied at 30	30 All
Tied at 40	Deuce

Bullseye!: Archery Scoring

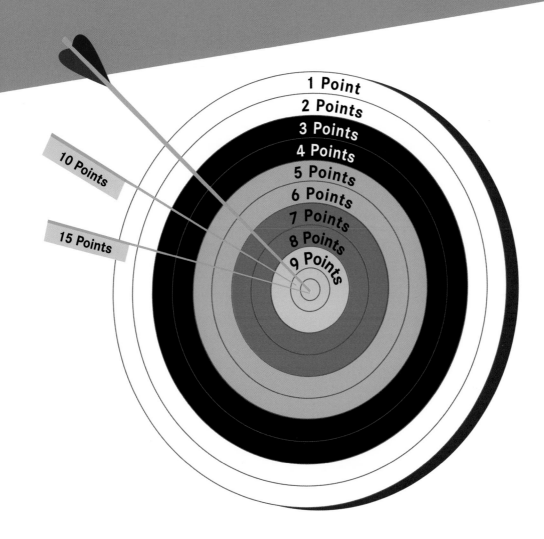

- If an arrow lands on a line between two rings, it gets the higher score.
- If an arrow gets stuck in another arrow, the second arrow gets the score of the first arrow. This is called a Robin Hood.

Swing, Hit, Run!: Baseball Scoring

BATTER	BALL	STRIKE	OUT
0 9	3	2	1

INNING	1	2	3	4	5	6	7	8	9	10	R	H	E
VISITOR	2	0	4	0	0	7	0	1	0	0	14	9	1
HOME	0	5	0	0	0	0	0	2	1	0	8	6	3

R (RUN)
when a batter crosses home plate, a run is awarded; a run is similar to a point, and the team with the most runs wins

E (ERROR)
a mistake by the **defensive** team that gives the batting team an advantage

H (HIT)
when a batter hits the ball and makes it to a base

Hole in One: Scoring in Golf

Golf is one of the few sports you win by scoring FEWER points than your opponents.

1. Each hole has an expected number of shots, called par.

2. Try to get the ball in the hole in or under par

3. A bogey is one shot over par

4. A double bogey is two shots over par.

5. Getting the ball in one shot under par is called a birdie.

6. Two shots under par is called an eagle.

Smallest Number Wins!

Running is another sport where the biggest number is not the best score. No matter how short or long a race is, the runner who finishes in the shortest amount of time is the winner.

5K

The 5K is a common road race. It is around 3 miles (5 km) long. Most runners complete a 5K in 30 to 40 minutes. The fastest 5K time in the world was 12 minutes, 49 seconds.

MARATHON

A marathon is 26.2 miles (42.2 kilometers) long. In 2022, 22,580 people ran in the Boston Marathon. Most runners complete a marathon in 4 to 5 hours. The winner of the 2022 Boston Marathon finished the race in just 2 hours, 6 minutes, and 51 seconds.

100-METER SPRINT

The 100-meter (330-foot) sprint is a common race. It is used in elementary school PE classes and in the Olympic Games. Most kids run the 100-meter sprint in around 14 to 15 seconds. The fastest 100-meter sprint took 9.63 seconds.

CHAPTER 2

How to Score More

Every sport has a basic way to score. Most sports also have ways to score even more. Players in individual sports can add extra moves or tricks. Most team sports have overtime or extra time. This allows more time to break a tie. Sometimes a soccer game is still tied after overtime. Then they have a **penalty shootout**. Baseball games have extra innings if there is a tie. In some sports, **fouls** also give teams a chance to score more.

Timeline of Changes in Sport Scoring

1875	Thirty extra minutes are added to the Football Association (FA) Cup Final soccer game. This secures a winner.
1920	A baseball game between the Brooklyn Robins and the Boston Braves lasts for 26 innings. The game ends in a tie. The sun went down and it was too dark to keep playing.
1920	An Olympic soccer match between the Netherlands and Sweden ends after 30 minutes of extra time.
1951	The Indianapolis Olympians and the Rochester Royals basketball teams play six overtime periods. This leads to the longest game in National Basketball Association (NBA) history.
1974	An extra 10-minute period of play is added to National Football League (NFL) games in the event of a tie.
1978	For the first time in soccer history, a World Cup final requires overtime to find a winner.
2008	The International Baseball Federation introduces a tiebreaker rule for extra innings. This helps avoid long games.
2017	For the first time in NFL history, the Super Bowl goes into overtime.

Extra Points in Football

EXTRA POINT
The kicker earns one point by kicking the ball through the goalposts.

TWO-POINT CONVERSION
The quarterback or another player earns two points by scoring another touchdown from the two-yard line.

SAFETY
The other team earns two points when a player is tackled or drops the ball in their own end zone.

Rams' Scoring by Type of Play in the 2020–21 Season

The Rams won the 2021 Super Bowl after winning 12 regular-season games and scoring 52 touchdowns (312 points). They scored their remaining 148 points using other plays.

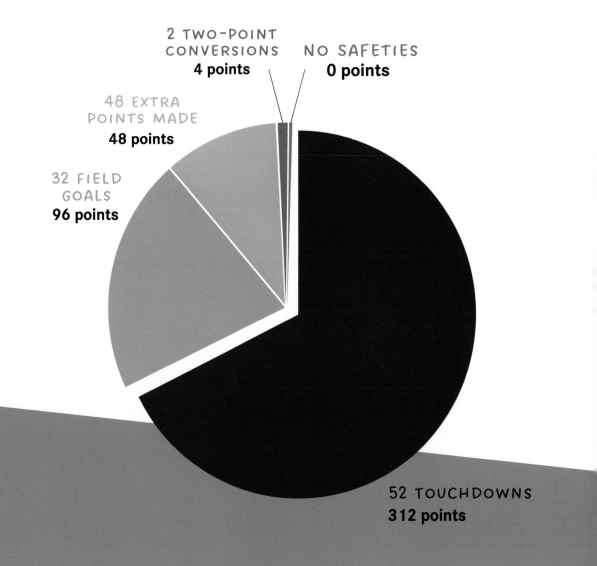

2 TWO-POINT CONVERSIONS
4 points

NO SAFETIES
0 points

48 EXTRA POINTS MADE
48 points

32 FIELD GOALS
96 points

52 TOUCHDOWNS
312 points

Three-Point Lines in Basketball

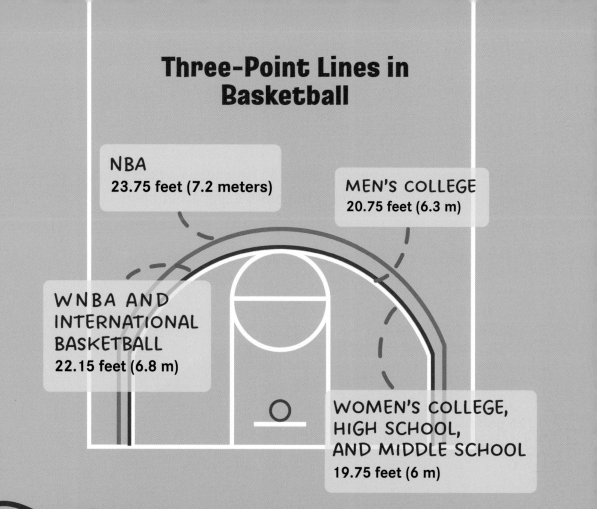

NBA
23.75 feet (7.2 meters)

MEN'S COLLEGE
20.75 feet (6.3 m)

WNBA AND INTERNATIONAL BASKETBALL
22.15 feet (6.8 m)

WOMEN'S COLLEGE, HIGH SCHOOL, AND MIDDLE SCHOOL
19.75 feet (6 m)

FAST FACTS

- The three-point line was added to the NBA game in 1979.

- There are usually two three-point lines on a basketball court. One is for men and one is for women.

- During the 2022–2023 Women's National Basketball Association (WNBA) season, the New York Liberty averaged 9.7 three-pointers made per game.

- Stephen Curry is tied for second-most three-point field goals made in a single game with 13. He is also tied for third, fourth, fifth, and sixth places, with 12, 11, 10, and 9.

Free Kick!

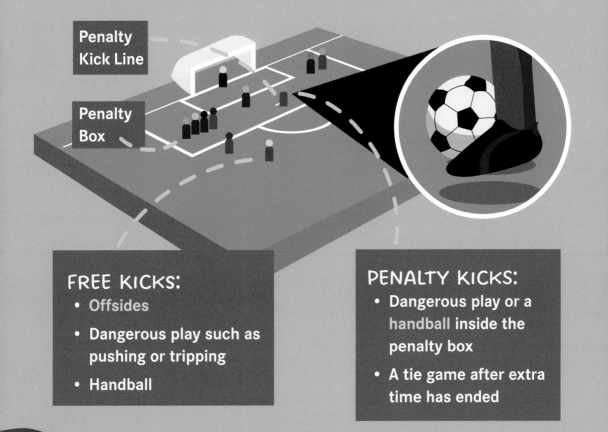

Penalty Kick Line

Penalty Box

FREE KICKS:
- Offsides
- Dangerous play such as pushing or tripping
- Handball

PENALTY KICKS:
- Dangerous play or a handball inside the penalty box
- A tie game after extra time has ended

FAST FACTS

Soccer isn't the only sport with a penalty shot. In hockey, a player might interfere with another player's scoring chance. So a penalty shot is awarded.

CHAPTER 3

Changing the Scoring Game

Technology has changed how people play sports. Many games are played in front of cameras. Some are even attached to drones. These "extra eyes" make it easy to stop and replay moments in games. A few big moments in sports history might have been different with modern tools. Some goals and touchdowns might never have been scored.

Instant Replay

1. THE PLAY
Was the player out of bounds?

2. REVIEW
The main referee looks at slowed-down videos to check.

3. DISCUSSION
All of the referees meet to discuss the play. Then the main referee talks to the coaches

4. DECISION
The main referee announces the final ruling.

Video Assistant Referee (VAR)

- There are four referees on the field during a FIFA soccer game.

  - For VAR, a team of three people are in a video room. They view film and review calls made by the main referee.

OFFSIDES

- FIFA first used VAR in 2018.

- In the 2022 World Cup, VAR reviewed every goal.

- New offsides technology was used in the 2022 World Cup. It can show if any part of a player is offsides, even a kneecap or the tip of a shoe.

Automatic Scoring in Fencing

Fencing is a sport where two people spar using sword-like weapons. Players get a point for each hit or contact between their sword and their opponent. Fencing was one of the sports in the first modern Olympic Games in 1896. At the 1936 Olympics, fencing also became the first sport in history to use electronic scoring.

The sword is attached to a long cable. The cable is attached to a small scoreboard. When one fighter makes a hit, the sword records a strike. That equals one point. The first player to 15 points is the winner.

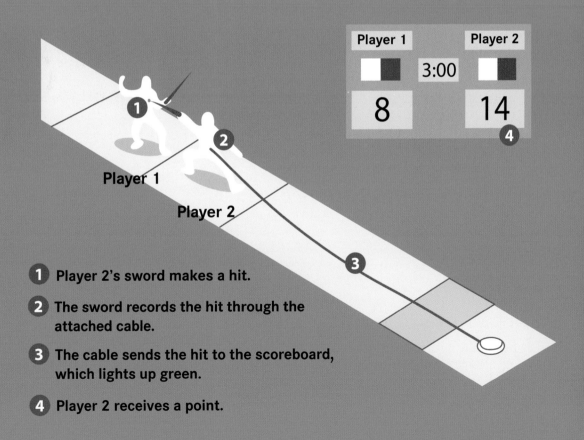

1 Player 2's sword makes a hit.

2 The sword records the hit through the attached cable.

3 The cable sends the hit to the scoreboard, which lights up green.

4 Player 2 receives a point.

CHAPTER 4

Who's on Top?

Most, first, fastest, best! Every sport has a list of records. Many of those records are based on scoring. Some records are set by teams. Others are set by individual athletes. Some records are even considered unbreakable.

Setting a record is a big deal for an athlete. It usually means they are the best in their sport. Breaking a record is a big deal, too. Working hard to score goals, touchdowns, or three-pointers makes a great athlete even more memorable.

Career Home Runs in Major League Baseball

Barry Bonds	**762**	Willie Mays	**660**
Hank Aaron	**755**	Ken Griffey Jr	**630**
Babe Ruth	**714**	Jim Thome	**612**
Albert Pujols	**703**	Sammy Sosa	**609**
Alex Rodriguez	**696**	Frank Robinson	**586**

2022, Sports Reference

Serena Willams, Greatest of All Time

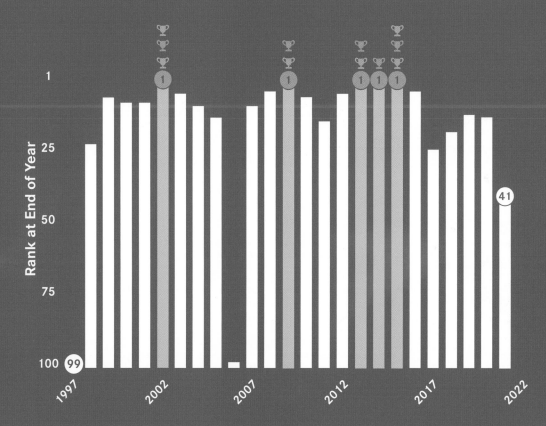

Serena Williams retired in 2022 after one of the most successful careers of any athlete in any sport.

- She won 23 major titles—the most ever by a woman.
- In 14 of the 26 years she played, her win percentage was 80 or higher.
- She beat 306 different players from 50 countries.
- She competed in four Olympics and won four gold medals.

2022, The Athletic

International Soccer's Top Goal-Scorers

Christine Sinclair

Team: Canada Women's
National Team

International Goals: 190

Time Range: 2000–2022

Cristiano Ronaldo

Team: Portugal
National Team

International Goals: 118

Time Range: 2003–2022

2022, Transfermarkt; 2022, Goal

Where Records Are Made

KAREEM ABDUL-JABBAR, BASKETBALL
38,387 career points in the NBA

RICKEY HENDERSON, BASEBALL
2,295 career runs in MLB

CA

TIGER WOODS, GOLF
20 career holes-in-one

DIANA TAURASI, BASKETBALL
9,693 career points in the WNBA

2022, Tiger Woods; 2021, NBA Media Ventures; 2021, Fadeaway World

STEPHEN CURRY, BASKETBALL
3,220 career three-pointers made in the NBA

ABBY WAMBACH, SOCCER
184 career goals for the US Women's National Team

WI

NY

PA

NJ

IL

OH

KY

MARY SLANEY, TRACK
fastest mile by an American woman (4 minutes, 16.71 seconds)

WILT CHAMBERLAIN, BASKETBALL
only NBA player in history to score 100 points in a single game

MS

JERRY RICE, FOOTBALL
208 career touchdowns in the NFL

TYSON GAY, TRACK
fastest men's 100-meter run (9.69 seconds)

Activity

How Many Ways to Score?

Materials Needed:

- This book
- Paper
- Writing utensil
- Calculator (if needed)

According to page 5, one of the highest-scoring NFL games of all time took place on November 27, 1966. The Washington Commanders beat the New York Giants 72–41.

You can guess how the teams scored those points. Use the infographic on page 16 to estimate how many touchdowns the Giants might have scored. First, divide their 41 points by 6.

$$41 / 6 = 6 \text{ with } 5 \text{ left over}$$

The remaining five points could have come from extra points.

The Giants also might have scored three touchdowns (3 x 6 = 18 points), six field goals (6 x 3 = 18), two two-point conversions (2 x 2 = 4), and one extra point (1 x 1 = 1), or:

$$18 + 18 + 4 + 1 = 41$$

Using this example and page 15, figure out at least three different ways the Commanders scored their game-winning 72 points. Make a pie chart like the one in the book for each scoring combination you come up with.

Learn More

Books

Connors, Kathleen. *Acadia National Park.* New York, NY: Gareth Stevens Publishing, 2016.

Cooke, Joanna. *The Sequoia Lives On.* San Francisco, CA: Yosemite Conservancy, 2018.

Graf, Mike. *My Yosemite: A Guide for Young Adventurers.* Berkeley, CA: Heyday, 2012.

Payne, Stephanie. *100 Things to See in the National Parks: Your Guide to the Most Popular Features of the US National Parks.* New York, NY: Adams Media, 2022.

On the Web

With an adult, learn more online with these suggested searches.

"Coastal Redwoods vs. Giant Sequoias." National Geographic Kids.

"Denali National Park and Preserve." National Geographic Kids.

"Shifting Shapes of Sandy Scapes." EO Kids.

"Virtual Tour of Yosemite Falls." Yosemite Mariposa County Tourism Bureau.

Glossary

diameter (dye-AH-muh-tuhr) the length of a straight line across the center of a circle

Eastern seaboard (EE-stuhrn SEE-bohrd) the region along the coast of the Atlantic Ocean

glaciers (GLAY-shuhrz) large buildups of snow, ice, rock, and sediment

old-growth forest (OLD-GROHTH FOHR-uhst) a forest with trees that are at least 150 years old

phenomenon (fih-NAH-muh-nahn) a rare or significant fact or event

refracted (rih-FRAK-tuhd) something that is bent and changed in direction, such as a ray of light

sand dunes (SAND DOONZ) mounds of sand formed by wind

summit (SUH-muht) the highest point of a mountain

Index

Acadia National Park, 6–9
activities, 30
Alaska, 26–29

Cadillac Mountain, 6–9
California, 16–19, 20–25
climate patterns, 9, 12, 15, 19, 28
Colorado, 10–15
creeks and streams, 15, 16, 18

Denali National Park and Preserve, 26–29, 30

El Capitan, 19

forest fires, 9
forests, 9, 20–25

General Sherman Tree, 20–25
giant sequoias, 20–25
glaciers, 28
Great Sand Dunes National Park, 10–15

hiking, 5, 8, 11, 15, 18, 29
Horsetail Fall, 19

Laumet, Antoine, 9
Lower Yosemite Fall, 16–17, 19

Maine, 6–9
McKinley, William, 26
Milky Way galaxy, 7
mountain climbing, 29
mountains
  Alaska Range and Denali, 26–29, 30
  Cadillac, 6–9
  El Capitan, 19
  Sangre de Cristo, 10–15
  Sierra Nevadas, 23
Mount Desert Island, 6–9

national parks, 5, 6–9, 10–15, 16–19, 20–25, 26–29
Native Americans, 9, 10, 23, 26, 27
natural light phenomena, 19, 28–29
Northern Lights, 29

old-growth forests, 20–25

redwoods, 23

sand dunes, 10–15
Sangre de Cristo Mountains, 10–15
Sequoia National Park, 20–25
Sierra Nevadas, 23
skygazing sites, 6–8, 29
sled dogs, 28–29
snow and ice melt, 15, 16, 18, 19, 28
Star Dune, 10, 11, 13
streams and creeks, 15, 16, 18

trees, 5, 8, 9, 20–25

Upper Yosemite Fall, 16–17, 18–19
Utes tribe, 10

Wabanaki tribes, 9
waterfalls, 15, 16–19
weather patterns, 9, 12, 15

Yosemite National Park, 16–19